ALL ABOUT MY DOG.

ALSO BY PHILIPP KEEL

All About Me.

All About Me—Millennium Edition.

All About Us.

Look at Me

All About My Cat.

Technicolor

ALL ABOUT MY DOG.

BY PHILIPP KEEL

BROADWAY BOOKS

NEW YORK

PRINTED IN THE UNITED STATES OF AMERICA

Visit our website at www.broadwaybooks.com

First edition published 2003

Based on an original design by Philipp Keel

Library of Congress Cataloging-in-Publication Data has been applied for.

Thanks to Liz Keel

ISBN 0-7679-1493-7

10 9 8 7 6 5 4 3 2 1

INTRODUCTION

Dogs offer us a kind of friendship that many people feel is the very best kind—one built upon an unconditional loyalty that we rarely experience with others. With their furry bodies, wagging tails, and playful eyes, dogs encourage us to be open and spontaneous, to be at ease with ourselves, and to approach the world with same unbridled enthusiasm and purity of heart that they themselves possess. They are always there to listen, they understand our moods, they help us to feel secure, and they never say no.

Your relationship with your dog is a daily affirmation not only of the powerful bond between animals and humans but of how easy it is, when we drop our guard, to let ourselves love and be loved. As you answer the questions in this book, you will be creating a cherished record of your dog's life and your years together that will reveal not only who you are as individuals but who you are together. It is my hope that the unique facts, opinions, and memories recorded will illuminate all the most special details that have made your lives so interesting and wonderful.

—Philipp Keel

CONTENTS

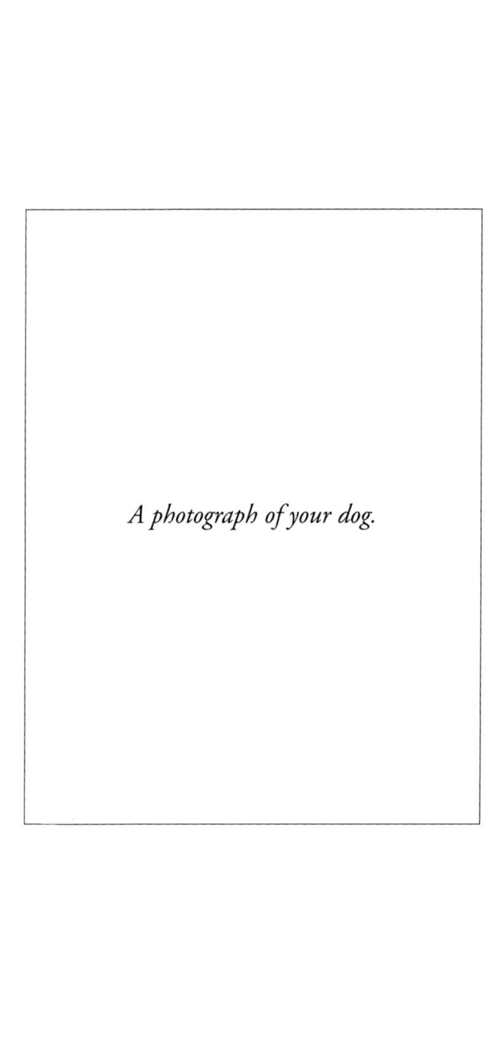

A photograph of your dog.

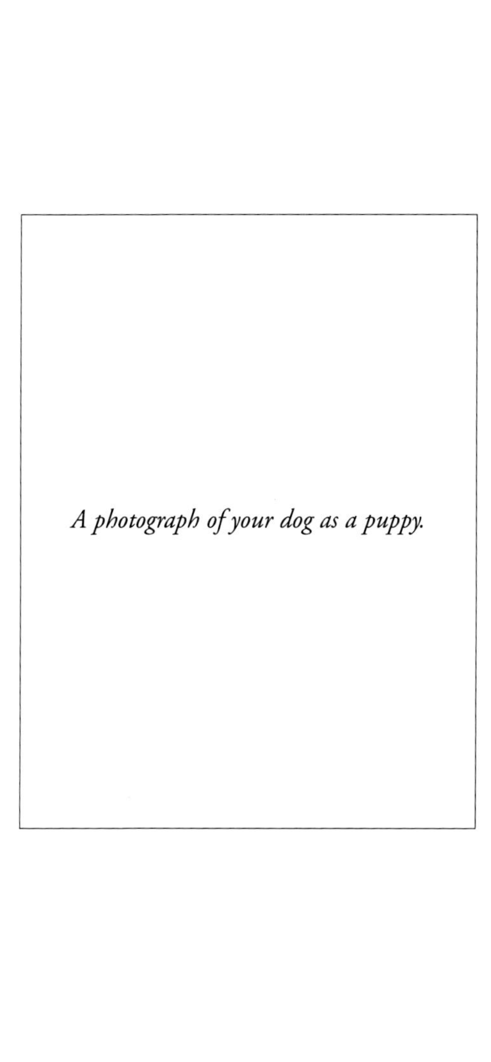

A photograph of your dog as a puppy.

ALL ABOUT MY DOG.

MY DOG

Why do you have a dog? ______________________________

Your dog's name: ______________________________

Date of birth (actual or estimated): ______________________________

Place of birth: ______________________________

Your dog is ( ) female. ( ) male.

Height: ______________________________

Weight: ______________________________

Fur color: ______________________________

Eye color: ______________________________

Distinct markings: ______________________________

Occupation: ______________________________

Education: ______________________________

Extracurricular activities: ______________________________

Awards: ______________________________

Describe your dog's appearance: ______________________________

MY DOG

What breed is your dog? ______________________________

( ) You found your dog. ( ) Your dog found you.

Why did you pick your dog's name? ______________________________

____

Your favorite nickname for your dog? ______________________________

If you had to choose a new name for your dog, what name would you pick from the following list?

( ) Tourist ( ) Jessica ( ) Falcon ( ) Dotcom ( ) Ralph
( ) Linear ( ) Händel ( ) Gucci ( ) Wow ( ) Leica
( ) Fynn ( ) Winner ( ) Liv ( ) Mario ( ) Hopper
( ) Kenya ( ) Tiber ( ) DJ ( ) Spring ( ) Emilie ( ) Mine
( ) Travolta ( ) Speedy ( ) Arnold ( ) FM ( ) Chrysler
( ) Hara ( ) Scorsese ( ) Pinkus ( ) Scotch ( ) Nasdaq
( ) Wasabe ( ) King ( ) Marzipan ( ) Weber ( ) Tiffy
( ) Madison ( ) Sark

Your dog is

( ) a princess. ( ) a tough guy. ( ) a tramp.
( ) a chicken. ( ) a role model. ( ) a pee wee.

Your dog is most like

( ) a friend. ( ) a partner. ( ) a guardian.
( ) a guest. ( ) a child.

MY DOG

Your dog is

( ) a city dog. ( ) a suburban dog. ( ) a country dog.

Your dog is

( ) an indoor dog. ( ) an outdoor dog.
( ) an indoor and outdoor dog.

Who is more loyal?

( ) You ( ) Your dog ( ) Your significant other

Your dog's biggest talent: ____________________

____

Your dog's astrological sign: ____________________

Do you think the sign matches her/his personality? ( ) Yes ( ) No

One word to describe your dog: ____________________

Your dog's motto: ____________________

____

Do you care about pedigree? ( ) Yes ( ) No

Have you always wanted your kind of dog? ( ) Yes ( ) No

If no, what kind of dog did you wish for? ______________________________

Why did you choose your dog? ______________________________

____

Three criteria for choosing a dog as a pet:

1 ______________________________

2 ______________________________

3 ______________________________

You got your dog

( ) as a puppy in a pet store.
( ) as a stray puppy from an animal shelter.
( ) as a puppy from the breeder.
( ) as a puppy from a newspaper ad.
( ) as a puppy from a neighbor or friend.
( ) as an adult in a pet store.
( ) as a stray adult from an animal shelter.
( ) as an adult from a newspaper ad.
( ) as an adult from a neighbor or friend.

Are you proud of your dog's appearance? ( ) Yes ( ) No

PEDIGREE OR MONGREL

Is she/he a pure breed? ( ) Yes ( ) No

If yes, who was the breeder? ______

What was her/his mother's name? ______

What was her/his father's name? ______

Your dog's weight when you got her/him: ______

Were there any champions in her/his lineage? ( ) Yes ( ) No

( ) Big dogs have more fun. ( ) Small dogs have more fun.

Something you think about mutts: ______

______

The most beautiful breed of dog: ______

The most stupid breed of dog: ______

The smartest breed of dog: ______

The meanest breed of dog: ______

The most dangerous breed of dog: ______

The most gentle breed of dog: ______

One breed with whom your dog doesn't like to associate: ____________________

One breed your dog loves to play with: ____________________

A breed of dog you would never want: ____________________

Do you find the movie *Best in Show* amusing? ( ) Yes ( ) No

Do you show your dog in competitions? ( ) Yes ( ) No

If yes, which shows? ____________________

Which show was the most memorable? ____________________

Awards your dog has won: ____________________

____

The award that made you the most proud: ____________________

If your dog doesn't appear in shows, your dog is

( ) still the winner.
( ) too smart to compete over beauty.
( ) mad at you for not entering contests.
( ) too old for that—but happier than ever.

Another animal your dog sometimes resembles: ____________________

CHARACTER

Your dog knows what she/he wants ( ) Yes ( ) No

Your dog is more like ( ) a Republican. ( ) a Democrat.

Athletically, your dog is most like which car? ______________________

What is your dog's guilty pleasure? ______________________

____

Your dog's three funniest habits:

1 ______________________

2 ______________________

3 ______________________

Three things your dog likes:

1 ______________________

2 ______________________

3 ______________________

Three things your dog dislikes:

1 ____

2 ____

3 ____

A sound that makes your dog excited: ____________________________

A sound that irritates your dog: ____________________________

A smell that makes your dog go crazy: ____________________________

Your dog is a wimp when it comes to: ____________________________

Something your dog is melodramatic about: ____________________________

What type of television entertainment does your dog prefer?

( ) Cartoons ( ) Silent movies ( ) War ( ) Sitcoms
( ) Documentaries ( ) Westerns ( ) Soap operas
( ) Action ( ) Comedies ( ) Dramas ( ) The Weather Channel
( ) Musicals ( ) News ( ) Talk shows ( ) Reality TV
( ) Game shows ( ) Cooking shows ( ) Commercials

Something that seems to make your dog depressed: ____________________________

Something that brings your dog joy: ____________________________

Which of the following musicians does your dog enjoy listening to the least?

( ) James Taylor ( ) Snoop Dogg ( ) Irving Berlin
( ) Enya ( ) Marilyn Manson ( ) Sting ( ) Johann Sebastian Bach
( ) The Kelly Family ( ) Carlos Santana ( ) Michael Jackson
( ) Shania Twain ( ) Ricky Martin ( ) Ella Fitzgerald
( ) Madonna ( ) Kenny G. ( ) Eminem ( ) Tom Jones
( ) The Velvet Underground ( ) Sinéad O'Connor
( ) Paul McCartney ( ) Earth, Wind & Fire
( ) Dimitri from Paris ( ) Eurythmics ( ) Neil Diamond
( ) Other: ____________________

Something that confuses your dog: ____________________

Your dog prefers ( ) men. ( ) women.

Your dog would most likely enjoy the works of which of the following authors? (pick one):

( ) Oscar Wilde ( ) Danielle Steele ( ) Ernest Hemingway
( ) Jane Austen ( ) Socrates ( ) James Joyce
( ) Helen Keller ( ) Lao-Tse ( ) Fyodor Dostoevsky
( ) Charles M. Schulz ( ) William Shakespeare

What historical figure does your dog remind you of? ____________________

Which character does your dog most closely resemble?

( ) Snoopy ( ) Marmaduke ( ) Clifford
( ) The Tramp from *Lady and the Tramp*
( ) Lady from *Lady and the Tramp* ( ) Goofy
( ) Pluto ( ) Scooby Doo ( ) Lassie ( ) Barkley

Your dog is ( ) too lazy. ( ) too active.

CHARACTER

As a master, you are

( ) too lazy. ( ) too busy. ( ) too catering.

Which of the following professions would best suit your dog?

( ) Rock Star ( ) Yoga Instructor ( ) Flight Attendant
( ) Social Worker ( ) Casino Host ( ) Firefighter
( ) Surfer ( ) Farmer ( ) Nurse ( ) Accountant
( ) Butler ( ) Teacher ( ) Conductor ( ) Art Dealer
( ) Gardener ( ) Actress/Actor ( ) Housewife ( ) Journalist
( ) CEO ( ) Artist ( ) Lifeguard

Your dog is moody. ( ) Yes ( ) No

Your dog gets angry when: ______________________________

When your dog is around other dogs, she/he tends to be

( ) a winner. ( ) a loser. ( ) outgoing. ( ) aloof.
( ) playful. ( ) shy. ( ) polite. ( ) rude. ( ) funny.
( ) snobby. ( ) crazy. ( ) peaceful.

Your dog gets frightened when: ______________________________

When your dog wants to be fed, she/he: ______________________________

When your dog wants to relax, she/he: ______________________________

When you disappoint your dog, she/he: ______________________________

Your dog is most playful when: ______________________________

CHARACTER

Your dog is fearless when: ____________________

Emotionally, your dog is most like which of your friends? ____________________

What makes your dog blush? ____________________

Something strangely human about your dog: ____________________

____

A DAY IN THE LIFE

Early Morning: ______________________________

8: ______________________________

9: ______________________________

10: ______________________________

11: ______________________________

Noon: ______________________________

1: ______________________________

2: ______________________________

3: ______________________________

4: ______________________________

5: ______________________________

6: ______________________________

7: ______________________________

8: ______________________________

9: ______________________________

10: ______________________________

Late Night: ______________________________

FETCHING FOR COMPLIMENTS

What makes a good dog? ______________________________

You say "good dog" ( ) enough. ( ) not enough.

Your dog's best quality: ______________________________

Your dog's worst quality: ______________________________

What is always wonderful about your dog? ______________________________

____

What is a little annoying about your dog? ______________________________

____

Your dog is most like which of the following characters?

( ) Bart Simpson ( ) Ivana Trump ( ) Tiger Woods
( ) Queen Elizabeth II ( ) Woody Allen ( ) Oprah
( ) Fred Astaire ( ) Whitney Houston ( ) Ozzy Osbourne
( ) Hillary Rodham Clinton ( ) Willie Nelson ( ) Elvis
( ) Julia Roberts ( ) Bill Gates ( ) Bo Derek
( ) David Letterman ( ) Martha Stewart
( ) Chevy Chase ( ) Shirley Temple ( ) Evel Knievel
( ) Luciano Pavarotti ( ) Judge Judy ( ) Emeril Lagasse
( ) Mahatma Gandhi

One compliment your dog likes to hear: ______________________________

One criticism your dog refuses to hear: ______________________________

FETCHING FOR COMPLIMENTS

Your dog makes people feel at ease. ( ) Yes ( ) No

Children cannot get enough of your dog. ( ) Yes ( ) No

What impresses you about your dog? ________________________________

What impresses other people about your dog? ________________________________

Do you praise your dog for no reason? ( ) Yes ( ) No

A compliment you often give your dog: ________________________________

HOME ALONE

Where do you and your dog live? ______________________________

____

How big is your dog's territory? ______________________________

Having a big dog in a small apartment is ______________________________

A place your dog would prefer to live: ______________________________

If you moved into a smaller space, your relationship with your dog would be

( ) worse. ( ) better. ( ) the same.

Your dog sometimes thinks living with you is quite uneventful. ( ) Probably ( ) No way

Your dog feels more comfortable when the house has just been cleaned. ( ) True ( ) False

Do you have a ritual with your dog when you are leaving the house? ( ) Yes ( ) No

Your dog enjoys being alone. ( ) Yes ( ) No

Do you leave the radio on for your dog when you go out? ( ) Yes ( ) No

If yes, what kind of music do you play for her/him? ______________________________

Do you feel guilty when you leave your dog alone? ( ) Yes ( ) No

HOME ALONE

How does your dog welcome you when you come home?

( ) She/he doesn't react. ( ) She/he slowly approaches you.
( ) She/he jumps on you. ( ) She/he barks and wags her/his tail.

How do you greet your dog when you come home? ______________________________

When you go on vacation, do you usually take your dog with you? ( ) Yes ( ) No

Your dog sitter is

( ) a paid professional.
( ) better at caring for your dog than you are.
( ) someone you can trust to take great care of your dog.
( ) someone who may or may not be regular with walks and feeding.
( ) the only one who will watch your dog for free.

Whom would your dog prefer to be taken care of? ______________________________

When you go away for a vacation, your good-byes with your dog most resemble which of the following movies?

( ) *Sophie's Choice* ( ) *Casablanca* ( ) *Titanic*
( ) *National Lampoon* ( ) *Some Like It Hot*
( ) *Dumb and Dumber* ( ) *The Three Amigos*
( ) *War of the Roses* ( ) *Kramer vs. Kramer*
( ) *Gone With the Wind* ( ) *Bambi* ( ) *Fargo*

HOME ALONE

Three things about your dog that make it hard to leave her/him behind:

1 ______________________________

2 ______________________________

3 ______________________________

Three things about your dog that make it easy to leave her/him behind:

1 ______________________________

2 ______________________________

3 ______________________________

When you are on vacation, how often do you think of your dog?

( ) Constantly ( ) Frequently ( ) Once a day
( ) Once or twice during the trip ( ) Never

Something you suspect your dog does when you are away: ______________________________

____

Does your dog act different when you come home after a trip? ( ) Yes ( ) No

If yes, how does it show? ______________________________

Your dog's ideal dinner: ______________________________

How often do you feed your dog by hand? ______________________________

Has your dog ever bitten the hand that feeds her/him? ( ) Yes ( ) No

Your dog's appetite is

( ) finicky, but she/he has good taste.
( ) not particular at all, she/he eats whatever you offer.
( ) spoiled, she/he whines until you hand-feed her/him people food.
( ) not fussy at all.

Has your dog ever rejected something you fed her/him? ( ) Yes ( ) No

If yes, what was it? ______________________________

Has your dog ever had a kosher meal? ( ) Yes ( ) No

You sometimes cook for your dog. ( ) Yes ( ) No

What is your dog's favorite people food? ______________________________

Your dog's favorite grocery store: ______________________________

How much do you spend a week on your dog's food? ______________________________

One word to describe your dog's table manners: ______________________________

Does your dog enjoy scavenging in the garbage? ( ) Yes ( ) No

BITE THE BONE

Something nonedible that your dog always puts in her/his mouth: ______________________

Something strange your dog once ate: ______________________

Who overfeeds your dog? ______________________

Someone who likes to give your dog treats: ______________________

Has anyone ever gotten your dog drunk? ( ) Yes ( ) No

If yes, what was your reaction? ______________________

You would love your dog to bite (choose one)

( ) Cher. ( ) an employee at Kinko's. ( ) all Teletubbies.
( ) Rush Limbaugh. ( ) your neighbor's children.
( ) any European. ( ) George W. Bush. ( ) every telemarketer.
( ) some lawyer. ( ) James Woods. ( ) your mother-in-law.
( ) Pope John Paul II. ( ) your hairdresser. ( ) Barney.
( ) Richard Simmons. ( ) your financial adviser. ( ) your boss.
( ) one of your exes. ( ) Dr. Laura Schlesinger. ( ) every terrorist.

WALKING THE DOG

The primary reason for walking your dog is

( ) natural needs. ( ) exercise. ( ) pleasure.

On a good day, you walk your dog

( ) once. ( ) twice. ( ) three times. ( ) four or more times.
( ) briefly. ( ) not at all.

A special place where you like to take your dog: ______________________________

Who keeps whom in shape?

( ) Your dog helps you to stay in shape.
( ) You help your dog to stay in shape.
( ) Neither—you are both lazy.

What captures your dog's attention on walks: ______________________________

When you pass someone else walking their dog on the street, you

( ) say hello to the owner. ( ) start talking to the other dog.
( ) command your dog to heel as you pass them.
( ) let your dog decide if she/he wants to interact with the other dog.
( ) hold your dog tightly on its leash and avoid eye contact.
( ) smile politely.

Do you like it when strangers pet your dog? ( ) Yes ( ) No

If no, are you overprotective of your dog? ( ) Yes ( ) No

Does your dog attract a lot of attention? ( ) Yes ( ) No

Who attracts more attention when you are out for a walk? ( ) You ( ) Your dog

Do you attract more attention when you are out with your dog than when you are alone? ( ) Yes ( ) No

Have you ever used your dog to meet someone? ( ) Yes ( ) No

The most interesting person you have met while walking your dog: ______________________

____

The most interesting thing you have seen while walking your dog: ______________________

____

Something you have learned about your neighbors while you were walking your dog: __________

____

Your dog park is more of a social event ( ) for owners. ( ) for dogs.

Your dog typically interacts with dogs who have owners you find (pick two)

( ) attractive. ( ) odd. ( ) professional.
( ) uninteresting. ( ) friendly. ( ) judgmental.
( ) talkative. ( ) rude. ( ) liberal. ( ) appealing.
( ) antisocial. ( ) good-natured. ( ) uneducated.
( ) sexy. ( ) helpful. ( ) pedestrian. ( ) superficial.
( ) conservative. ( ) arrogant. ( ) strange.
( ) funny. ( ) boring. ( ) fresh.

More times than not, your dog chooses to play with dogs who have owners

( ) you would befriend. ( ) you would not befriend.

PLAYTIME

How often do you play with your dog?

( ) Every day ( ) At least once a week ( ) When you feel like it
( ) Not enough ( ) Unfortunately, hardly ever

Do you play enough with your dog?

( ) You wish it were less. ( ) You wish it were more.

List some of your dog's toys: ______________________________

____

The toy your dog loves best: ______________________________

You've played dress-up with your dog. ( ) Yes ( ) No

Do you dance with your dog holding her/his paws? ( ) Yes ( ) No

Playing with your dog makes you feel young. ( ) Yes ( ) No

Your dog's yawn is ______________________________

Your dog is in a cuddling mood

( ) when she/he has just been fed.
( ) after coming home from playing outside.
( ) when you stroke her/his fur.
( ) whenever she/he feels like it.
( ) only when sleepy.

Your dog prefers to lounge in

( ) the kitchen. ( ) the living room. ( ) the dining room.
( ) the computer room. ( ) the children's or guest room.
( ) the basement. ( ) the attic. ( ) your bedroom.

Where does your dog sleep? ______________________________

Do you like your dog to sleep in bed with you? ( ) Yes ( ) No

Do you cover your dog at night? ( ) Yes ( ) No

If yes, with what? ______________________________

Do you kiss your dog good night? ( ) Yes ( ) No

If yes, where do you kiss your dog good night? ______________________________

Your dog's bedtime habit: ______________________________

____

Describe your dog's sleep in one word: ______________________________

When sleeping, your dog resembles: ______________________________

Does your dog make sounds when she/he sleeps? ( ) Yes ( ) No

What does your dog dream about? ______________________________

____

How does your dog get you out of bed in the morning? ______________________________

____

What does your dog expect from you in the morning?

( ) She/he wants to be fed.
( ) She/he wants to play.
( ) She/he wants to go for a walk.
( ) She/he wants you to leave her/him alone.
( ) She/he wants to get in your bed.

A photograph of your dog sleeping.

One word that describes your dog's bark: ______________________________

The most common reason your dog barks: ______________________________

A neighbor your dog enjoys barking at: ______________________________

Have you ever barked at your dog? ( ) Yes ( ) No

When your dog wags her/his tail, it means ______________________________

When your dog yelps, it means ______________________________

When your dog woofs, it means ______________________________

When your dog howls, it means ______________________________

When your dog growls, it means ______________________________

When your dog whimpers, it means ______________________________

When your dog whines, it means ______________________________

Which word do you use most often when speaking to your dog?

( ) No ( ) Heel ( ) Good ( ) Yes ( ) Hello ( ) Sit
( ) Bad ( ) Good-bye ( ) Come ( ) Stay ( ) Hey
( ) Don't ( ) Why ( ) There ( ) Fetch ( ) Wait

Three words your dog understands:

1 ______________________________

2 ______________________________

3 ______________________________

Does your dog sometimes mix up the words "yes" and "no"? ( ) Yes ( ) No

If yes, do you think she/he secretly knows the difference? ( ) Yes ( ) No

Do you curse at your dog? ( ) Yes ( ) No

Does your dog usually understand what you want? ( ) Yes ( ) No

Do you usually understand what your dog wants? ( ) Yes ( ) No

Someone or something your dog loves to bark at: ______________________________

Who cleans up after your dog? ____________________

How long did it take you to housebreak your dog? ____________________

Did the housebreaking process ever make you like your dog less? ( ) Yes ( ) No

Does your dog ever have an "accident"? ( ) Yes ( ) No

If yes, your dog is

( ) ashamed. ( ) concerned. ( ) mocking. ( ) oblivious.

The most notorious accident your dog has ever had: ____________________

Has your dog ever gone to the bathroom in a place that embarrassed you? ( ) Yes ( ) No

If yes, where? ____________________

Your dog's favorite place to pee: ____________________

A place your dog is scared to pee: ____________________

If you live in a place where there are curbing laws, do you sometimes break them? ( ) Yes ( ) No

How would you feel, if your state government eliminated the "Curb Your Dog" laws? __________

____

To your dog, fire hydrants are

( ) the holy grail.   ( ) something worth sniffing.
( ) inconsequential.

When your dog heeds nature's call, you

( ) can't help but look to see what your dog has done.
( ) always look away.
( ) have to deal with it everyday because you live in a city and there are curbing laws.
( ) don't mind cleaning up after your dog, it's natural.
( ) praise the invention of the Pooper Scooper.

Do you use a Pooper Scooper™?   ( ) Yes   ( ) No

Name someone you know who would never clean up after a dog: ______________________

Who is the most obedient?

( ) Your dog   ( ) Your significant other   ( ) Your kids

Have you ever considered sending your dog to obedience school?   ( ) Yes   ( ) No

If you sent your dog to obedience school, how did she/he change? ______________________

____

How much money have you spent on your dog's training? ______________________

Three important things you had to teach your dog:

1 ____________________

2 ____________________

3 ____________________

Three things your dog knew without being taught:

1 ____________________

2 ____________________

3 ____________________

The most meaningful thing your dog has damaged: ____________________

The most expensive thing your dog has damaged: ____________________

One moment when you wanted to get rid of your dog: ____________________

Your dog reacts to commands in the following languages:

( ) English ( ) Spanish ( ) Hebrew ( ) Chinese
( ) Japanese ( ) Russian ( ) Italian ( ) French
( ) Portuguese ( ) Arabic ( ) Swedish ( ) German
( ) Other: ____________________

When you use the "sit" command, about how long does your dog stay seated?

( ) A few seconds ( ) Thirty seconds ( ) One minute
( ) It varies ( ) As long as you want her/him to sit
( ) Until you give her/him a treat

A command your dog will always disobey: __________

One naughty thing your dog does behind your back: __________

A trick your dog knows: __________

Something unusual that you have taught your dog: __________

Your dog can walk on her/his hind legs. ( ) Yes ( ) No

A service you wish you could train your dog to perform: __________

Something you wish your dog would fetch for itself: __________

One thing you have been unable to teach your dog, no matter how hard you try: __________

____

One thing you should have never taught your dog: __________

You yell at the top of your voice when your dog: __________

If you yell at your dog, she/he: __________

If you yell at your dog, do you feel guilty afterward? ( ) Yes ( ) No

DOGMATIC

Have you ever spanked your dog? ( ) Yes ( ) No

If yes, why? ____

As an authority figure, you most closely resemble:

( ) Napoleon ( ) Your mother ( ) Your father
( ) Nelson Mandela ( ) Mr. Rogers ( ) Hulk Hogan
( ) Beaver Cleaver ( ) Joan Crawford ( ) Joseph Stalin
( ) Martina Navratilova ( ) The Dalai Lama
( ) The Germans ( ) Madonna ( ) Genghis Khan
( ) Margaret Thatcher ( ) Mother Teresa
( ) Fidel Castro ( ) Carol Brady ( ) Siegfried or Roy

Your dog wouldn't dare to: ____

You could not live with a dog who: ____

How would your dog react if a burglar broke into your home? ____________________

____

Your dog should fight if: ____

Would you keep your dog if she/he bit someone? ( ) Yes ( ) No

When your dog does something well, she/he has a sense of pride in her/his success. ( ) Yes ( ) No

If your dog had gone to college, what would she/he have studied? ____________________

____

POLITICS

Does your dog think you are fair? ( ) Yes ( ) No

Every dog is born with the following three rights:

1 ______________________________

2 ______________________________

3 ______________________________

Does your dog have the right not to be spayed or neutered? ( ) Yes ( ) No

How do you think your dog feels when she/he is on a leash? ______________________________

____

How do you feel when your dog is on a leash? ______________________________

____

Would you put a muzzle on your dog? ( ) Yes ( ) No

You would never have your dog put to sleep, unless: ______________________________

A dog should not be treated like a human. ( ) You agree. ( ) You disagree.

What do you do if your dog is sitting where you want to sit? ______________________________

____

Are you your dog's best friend? ( ) Yes ( ) No

If no, who is your dog's best friend? ______________________________

Is your dog your best friend? ( ) Yes ( ) No

You care

( ) more about your dog.
( ) more about people (family not included).

Your relationship with your dog is the best you have ever had. ( ) Yes ( ) No

Do you say "I love you" to your dog? ( ) Yes ( ) No

Does your dog sense what mood you are in? ( ) Yes ( ) No

If yes, what does she/he do when you feel

lonely: ______________________________

sad: ______________________________

moody: ______________________________

angry: ______________________________

afraid: ______________________________

crazy: ______________________________

nervous: ______________________________

careless: ______________________________

romantic: ______________________________

concerned: ______________________________

happy: ______________________________

Without your dog, you would be

( ) depressed. ( ) fine. ( ) less of a person. ( ) lonely.
( ) the same. ( ) inactive. ( ) unscheduled. ( ) bored.
( ) liberated. ( ) less childish. ( ) a world traveler.
( ) less healthy. ( ) someone you are not.
( ) unhappy. ( ) out of your mind.

Your dog helped you by: ______________________________

On which days of the week does your dog cheer you up most?

( ) Sunday ( ) Monday ( ) Tuesday ( ) Wednesday
( ) Thursday ( ) Friday ( ) Saturday

Generally, you spend

( ) enough time with your dog.
( ) not enough time with your dog.
( ) too much time with your dog.

Who gets the most attention in your household?

( ) Your dog ( ) Your TV ( ) Your bills
( ) Your refrigerator ( ) Your telephone

Who is the best listener?

( ) Your dog ( ) Your significant other ( ) Your mother

What do you tell your dog that you don't tell anyone else? ______________________________

____

Who is the most predictable?

( ) Your dog ( ) Your significant other ( ) You

What is the most unusual gift your dog has ever brought to you? ______________________

What does your dog hide from you? ____

What do you hide from your dog? ____

Do you feel embarrassed when your dog sees you naked? ( ) Yes ( ) No

What do you believe your dog thinks when she/he sees you naked? ____________________

____

What do you and your dog disagree on? ____

____

What you absolutely refuse to share with your dog: ______________________________

How does your dog fight with you? ______________________________

A moment when you were afraid and your dog made you feel protected: ______________________________

____

A dangerous situation when your dog saved you: ______________________________

____

If your house was burning and you couldn't find your dog, you would

( ) leave your dog behind and evacuate immediately.
( ) remain in the inferno, calling for your dog, until the last possible second.
( ) escape and inform the firemen that your dog is still inside.
( ) risk your life and run through the raging fire looking for your dog.
( ) not think twice about your dog—you would be too concerned that you and/or your family got out of the building safely.

How much money would it take for you to sell your dog?

( ) You would never sell your dog. ( ) $50 ( ) $5,000
( ) $25,000 ( ) $100,000 ( ) $250,000 ( ) $1,000,000
( ) You would give her/him away for free, but no one is interested.

Do you think you have too many pictures of your dog? ( ) Yes ( ) No

When you take a group portrait of your family, do you include your dog? ( ) Yes ( ) No

Do you think your dog is adopting your personality? ( ) Yes ( ) No

If yes, how does it show? ______________________________

Do you think you are adopting your dog's personality? ( ) Yes ( ) No

If yes, how does it show? ______________________________

Do you sometimes wish you could switch roles with your dog? ( ) Yes ( ) No

If yes, why? ______________________________

Is your dog lucky to have you as an owner? ( ) Yes ( ) No

If yes, why is she/he lucky? ______________________________

What is most special about the relationship between you and your dog ______________________________

____

If you couldn't have a dog, what animal (even if owning it as a pet is not realistic) would you like to have? ______________________________

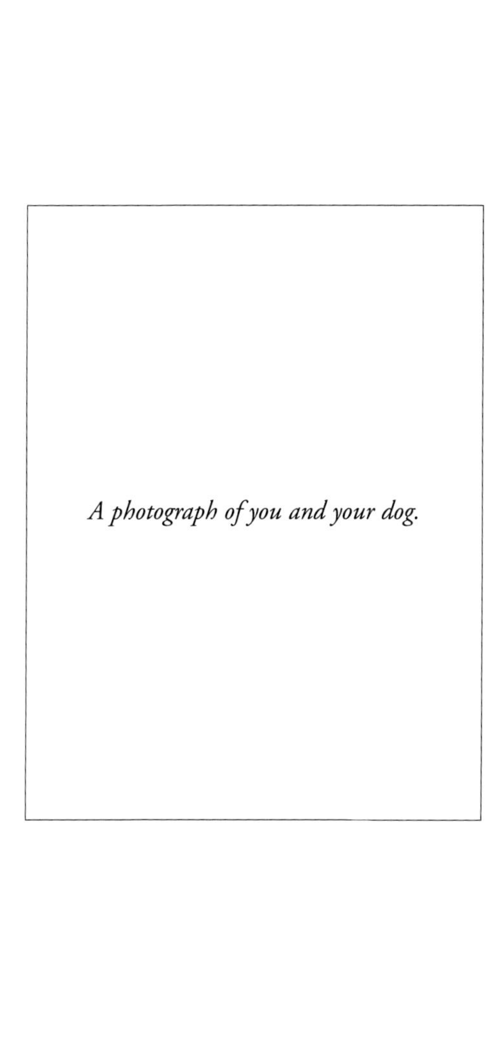
A photograph of you and your dog.

VANITY FUR

Does your dog enjoy luxury? ( ) Yes ( ) No

If yes, what kind of luxury? ______________________________

Your dog is spoiled. ( ) Yes ( ) No

What is your dog's most attractive feature? ______________________________

What is your dog's least attractive feature? ______________________________

Which of your dog's odors disturbs you more? ( ) Fur ( ) Breath

How often do you bathe your dog? ______________________________

How much time per week do you spend grooming your dog's fur?

( ) 10 minutes ( ) 30 minutes ( ) 1 hour ( ) 5 hours

How long is your dog's hair? ______________________________

Have you ever trimmed your dog's fur? ( ) Yes ( ) No

Does your dog let you clip her/his nails? ( ) Yes ( ) No

Your dog's beauty regimen: ______________________________

____

How often does your dog go to the groomer?

( ) never ( ) only on special occasions ( ) once a month
( ) once a week ( ) more than once a week

Does she/he enjoy it? ( ) Yes ( ) No

Have you ever taken your dog to a dog spa? ( ) Yes ( ) No

If yes, how often? ____________________

List any dog beauty treatments that you find ridiculous: ____________________

Would you ever get your dog a manicure? ( ) Yes ( ) No

Who is better looking?

( ) You in human society ( ) Your dog in the dog world
( ) You both look fantastic

Your dog's looks most closely resemble those of:

( ) Salman Rushdie. ( ) Cindy Crawford. ( ) you.
( ) Little Richard. ( ) Andy Warhol. ( ) John Lennon.
( ) Albert Einstein. ( ) Mikhail Gorbachev.
( ) Catherine Zeta Jones. ( ) Barry White. ( ) Bill Maher.
( ) Venus Williams. ( ) Buddha. ( ) Peter Jennings.
( ) Donatella Versace. ( ) Alfred Hitchcock. ( ) Bill Clinton.
( ) David Copperfield. ( ) Jacqueline Kennedy Onassis.
( ) Dolly Parton. ( ) Boris Karloff. ( ) Michael Jackson.
( ) Andre Agassi. ( ) Joan Rivers. ( ) Etta James.
( ) Mao Zedong. ( ) Mariah Carey.

Do you ever feel that your dog costs too much money? ( ) Yes ( ) No

How much do you spend a year on your dog's care? ____________________

If you couldn't have a dog, what would you buy with that money? ______________________

____

The part of your dog's care you don't mind paying for: ______________________

The part of your dog's care you do mind paying for: ______________________

Have you ever spent a ridiculous amount of money that
you didn't have on something for your dog? ( ) Yes ( ) No

If yes, what? ______________________________________

Have you run into severe financial situation because of your dog? ( ) Yes ( ) No

If yes, why? ______________________________________

Have you ever done something for your dog that you were
embarrassed to tell others? ( ) Yes ( ) No

If yes, what? ______________________________________

Does your dog ever wear clothes? ( ) Yes ( ) No

If yes, list the items in your dog's wardrobe: ______________________

____

VANITY FUR

You prefer photographs of your dog

( ) in action. ( ) posed. ( ) in costumes.
( ) with family members. ( ) sleeping.

Your dog is a great performer when: ______________________________

____

Has your dog ever appeared in any newspapers or magazines? ( ) Yes ( ) No

If yes, which one and why? ______________________________

Has your dog ever been on television? ( ) Yes ( ) No

If yes, why? ______________________________

Something you love to get for your dog: ______________________________

DOGTOR FREUD

What does your dog think of the world? ________________________________

____

What does your dog think of you? ________________________________

____

Is your dog happy? ( ) Yes ( ) No

If no, why not? ________________________________

What kind of animal does your dog think she/he is? ________________________________

Your dog wishes that: ________________________________

Your dog's biggest secret: ________________________________

What is your dog's biggest inner conflict? ________________________________

Your dog's biggest complaint about humans: ________________________________

Which of the following sayings would hurt your dog's feelings the most?

( ) It's a dog-eat-dog world.
( ) Not even a dog would have eaten that!
( ) She's ugly like a dog!
( ) How can anyone live with a dog?
( ) He's dumb as a dog!
( ) Yuck, you smell like a dog!
( ) Wow, you act like a dog in heat.

Can you think like a dog? ( ) Yes ( ) No

Your dog's animal instincts are

( ) long gone. ( ) dormant.
( ) acute and helpful when looking for food.
( ) guard sharp when there is a stranger on the property.
( ) to eat and sleep. ( ) impressive.

Your dog is more ( ) pessimistic. ( ) optimistic.

When you let your dog run loose at the park, do you feel that you are improving your relationship by giving her/him freedom? ( ) Yes ( ) No

What is your dog neurotic about? ______________________________

The source of your dog's anxiety is (choose as many as apply):

( ) traumatic puppyhood experiences.
( ) your mercurial behavior. ( ) poor training.
( ) her/his breed disposition. ( ) children.
( ) lack of attention. ( ) fear of doggie sweaters.
( ) that she/he was a stray.
( ) that she/he was the runt of the litter.
( ) that she/he is a mutt. ( ) fear of cats.
( ) that you expect her/him to be perfect.
( ) the inconsistency in your care schedule.
( ) too long a wait in between meals.
( ) bothered by other household pets.

Does your dog often suffer from separation anxiety? ( ) Yes ( ) No

If yes, how does it show? ______________________________

Does your dog often cry? ( ) Yes ( ) No

If yes, what is she/he crying about? ______________________________

What does your dog think is really funny? ______________________________

Do you think it hurts your dog's feelings when you make her/him get off the couch? ( ) Yes ( ) No

What is your dog afraid of? ______________________________

A dramatic change in your dog's behavior was caused by ______________________________

A dramatic change in your dog's weight was caused by ______________________________

Have you ever feared your dog could turn on you and seriously harm you? ( ) Yes ( ) No

Does your dog have any real problems? ( ) Yes ( ) No

If yes, what are they? ______________________________

____

Most of the time you feel you and your dog are

( ) on the same team. ( ) not on the same team.

Is your dog a substitute for something you are missing in your life? ( ) Yes ( ) No

If yes, try to describe what you are missing in one word: ______________________________

Your dog's favorite destination: ______________________________

Describe your dog in a traveling crate or kennel cab: ______________________________

Have you ever drugged your dog before traveling with her/him? ( ) Yes ( ) No

Traveling with your dog for long distances is

( ) fun. ( ) dangerous to your dog's health. ( ) natural.
( ) stupid. ( ) a hassle. ( ) cruel. ( ) adventureous.

Were you ever afraid a trip with your dog might threaten her/his life? ( ) Yes ( ) No

Has your dog ever been on an airplane? ( ) Yes ( ) No

If yes, how many times? ______________________________

If yes, your dog was ( ) in the cabin. ( ) in the cargo compartment.

If your dog traveled in the cabin, was she/he scared during takeoff? ( ) Yes ( ) No

If your dog was stowed in the cargo compartment, how did you feel about that during the flight?

____

Was your dog angry with you when you met her/him at the baggage claim? ( ) Yes ( ) No

Has your dog ever been on a train? ( ) Yes ( ) No

Would your dog enjoy riding in a convertible? ( ) Yes ( ) No

If you drive with your dog, where does she/he sit? ______________________________

Does your dog enjoy a barbeque at a rest area? ( ) Yes ( ) No

Your dog's behavior when you stop at a scenic point: ______________________________

Your dog appreciates visiting

( ) national monuments. ( ) drive-throughs.
( ) museums. ( ) national parks. ( ) malls.
( ) antique fairs. ( ) theme parks. ( ) diners.

Your dog most appreciates driving

( ) over a mountain. ( ) through a forest.
( ) across a river. ( ) through a city.
( ) along the sea. ( ) through a desert.
( ) across the Great Plains. ( ) through a tunnel.

When you stay in hotels with your dog, do you seek hotels that welcome animals or do you try to sneak your dog in? ______________________________

Have you ever been caught smuggling your dog to the room? ( ) Yes ( ) No

How many states has your dog seen? ______________________________

What was your dog's favorite state? ______________________________

List the countries your dog has visited: ______________________________

____

Does your dog seem to like different cultures? ( ) Yes ( ) No

A culture you think your dog would love to be a part of: ______________________

Have you ever lost your dog during a vacation? ( ) Yes ( ) No

Your dog's reaction to snow: ______________________

Your dog's reaction to rain: ______________________

What was your dog's reaction when she/he saw the sea for the first time? ______________________

At the beach, your dog prefers ( ) the sand. ( ) the water.

If your dog has never left home, why don't you travel with your dog? ______________________

____

A place you think your dog would like to travel to: ______________________

Your dog's ideal vacation: ______________________

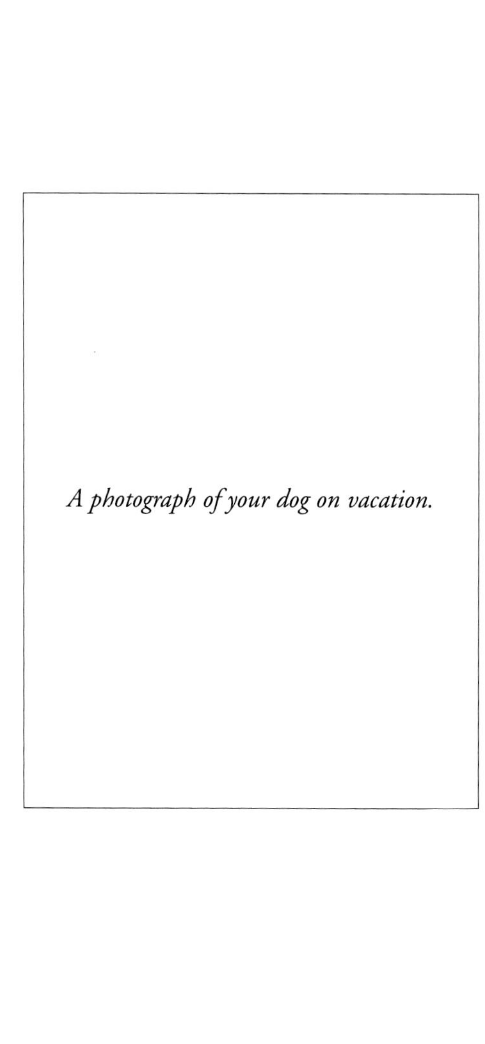
A photograph of your dog on vacation.

FAVORITES

Your dog's favorite time of day: ______________________________

Your dog's favorite waste of time: ______________________________

Your dog's favorite piece of furniture: ______________________________

Your dog's favorite way to tease you: ______________________________

Your dog's favorite form of entertainment: ______________________________

Which is your dog's favorite holiday?

( ) Hanukkah ( ) Christmas ( ) Kwanzaa
( ) New Year's Day ( ) Martin Luther King, Jr. Day
( ) Valentine's Day ( ) Holi ( ) Passover ( ) Easter
( ) Cinco de Mayo ( ) Memorial Day
( ) Independence Day ( ) Labor Day
( ) Rosh Hashanah ( ) Ramadan ( ) Halloween
( ) Veterans' Day ( ) Thanksgiving ( ) Birthdays
( ) Other: ______________________

Your dog's favorite treat: ______________________________

Your dog's favorite artist: ______________________________

Your dog's favorite music or singer: ______________________________

Your dog's favorite TV show: ______________________________

Your dog's favorite movie: ______________________________

FAVORITES

Your dog's favorite celebrity: ______

What does your dog enjoy most?

( ) Socializing with other dogs ( ) Socializing with other pets
( ) Socializing with humans ( ) Being alone with toys
( ) Being alone in nature

Your dog's favorite place to nap: ______

Your dog's favorite place to think: ______

Something inappropriate your dog likes to sniff: ______

Places your dog likes to scratch: ______

A strange place where your dog likes to relax: ______

The sport your dog most enjoys playing or watching: ______

Where does your dog most like to be petted: ______

Your dog's favorite indoor hobby: ______

Your dog's favorite outdoor hobby: ______

FAVORITES

Your dog's favorite activity is

( ) fetching a stick or a ball. ( ) pulling on a rope.
( ) catching a Frisbee. ( ) jumping in the water.
( ) running. ( ) chasing children. ( ) barking at seniors.
( ) digging. ( ) biting squeaky toys. ( ) eating.
( ) harassing guests. ( ) annoying you.
( ) Other: ______________________

Your dog's favorite thing to bite: ______________________

Your dog's favorite thing to catch: ______________________

The best day of your dog's life: ______________________

Your dog's hero: ______________________

Your dog's favorite dog: ______________________

SOCIAL MATTERS

Who are your dog's real friends? ______________________________

Does your dog have a boyfriend or girlfriend? ( ) Yes ( ) No

If yes, who? ______________________________

Has your dog ever had sex? ( ) Yes ( ) No

If yes, did it change her/his attitude? ( ) Yes ( ) No

Has your dog ever had puppies? ( ) Yes ( ) No

Do you have other animals in your home besides your dog? ( ) Yes ( ) No

If yes, what is their relationship like? ______________________________

____

Which of the following pets does your dog dislike?

( ) Dog ( ) Cat ( ) Rabbit ( ) Fish
( ) Guinea pig ( ) Rat ( ) Bird ( ) Hamster ( ) Mouse
( ) Lizard ( ) Cow ( ) Horse
( ) Other: ______________________________

Your dog is most social

( ) with you. ( ) with children. ( ) with other dogs.
( ) with strangers. ( ) with cats.

Your dog is most antisocial

( ) with you. ( ) with children. ( ) with other dogs.
( ) with strangers. ( ) with cats.

A member of your family or a friend with whom your dog loves to spend time: ______________

____

A member of your family or a friend whom your dog ignores the most: ____________________

____

When you have company, your dog tends to act

( ) discreet. ( ) pushy. ( ) insulted. ( ) welcoming.
( ) rude. ( ) humble. ( ) territorial. ( ) casual.
( ) polite.

If your dog sniffs your guests in an uncomfortable way, you

( ) yell at your dog.
( ) let her/him get to know your guest better.
( ) pull her/him away and apologize to your guest.
( ) say "don't worry, she/he does that to everyone."
( ) ignore it and keep on talking.

If a guest doesn't like your dog, you

( ) don't like your guest.
( ) put your dog in another room.
( ) let your dog bark and sniff.
( ) show your guest how great your dog is.
( ) feel insulted—any guest of yours should accept your dog.
( ) think people should say something only if they are allergic.

Try to describe the difference between "dog people" and "cat people" in one sentence:

Cat people are: ____

Dog people are: ____

Has anyone ever had an allergic reaction to your dog? ( ) Yes ( ) No

If yes, who? ____

How does it make you feel when your dog is overly affectionate with a guest? ____________

Someone who is very strict with your dog: ____________________________

Someone your dog enjoys flirting with: ____________________________

Would you date someone who didn't like dogs? ( ) Yes ( ) No

Would you break up with someone if your dog didn't get along with his/her dog? ( ) Yes ( ) No

Have you ever ended a relationship with someone because she/he didn't like your dog? ( ) Yes ( ) No

Do you mind your dog being in the same room when you are intimate with someone? ( ) Yes ( ) No

If yes, why? ____

Do you mind your dog visiting you in the bathroom? ( ) Yes ( ) No

If yes, why? ______________________________

Does your dog have any enemies in your neighborhood (including people)? ( ) Yes ( ) No

Whom do you suspect secretly feeds your dog? ______________________________

Your neighbor's property is off limits. ( ) Yes ( ) No

Has your dog ever been attacked by another animal? ( ) Yes ( ) No

If yes, what happened? ______________________________

Has your dog ever attacked another animal? ( ) Yes ( ) No

If yes, what happened? ______________________________

Whom would you like your dog to meet? ______________________________

ALL IN ALL

One word to describe your dog's future: ______________________________

What is going to be your dog's legacy? ______________________________

What is the most important thing you have learned from your dog? ______________

Tell someone who doesn't like dogs one important thing that she/he should know: ________

____

Your most beautiful memory when your dog was a puppy: ____________________

Your most special memory with your dog so far: __________________________

A moment when your dog made you really proud: __________________________

What would you like to do for your dog at least once in her/his life: ______________

____

When your dog passes away, you will: ______________________________

What do you wish for your dog? __________________________________

What do you wish for your dog to wish for you? ________________________

Your dog is better than the average dog. ( ) Of course. ( ) You wish.

Dogs are better than cats. ( ) Yes ( ) No

Your dog is the best thing that ever happened to you. ( ) Yes ( ) No

Your dog's pawprint.

Medical Record: ____

____

____

Feeding Notes: ____

____

____

Date of neuter: ____

Pregnancies: ____

____

____

Date of first birth: ____

Number of puppies in the litter: ____

Names, identifying colors, and markings of each puppy: ____________________

____

____

____

____

Date of second birth: ____________________

Number of puppies in the litter: ____________________

Names, identifying colors, and markings of each puppy: ____________________

____

____

____

____

PHOTOS

NOTES

PHOTOS

N O T E S